A BLUE BANNER BIOGRAPHY

Justin Timberlake

Kathleen Tracy

Mitchell Lane
PUBLISHERS

P.O. Box 196
Hockessin, Delaware 19707
Visit us on the web: www.mitchelllane.com
Comments? email us: mitchelllane@mitchelllane.com

Mitchell Lane PUBLISHERS

Printing   1   2   3   4   5   6   7   8   9

Blue Banner Biographies

Akon	Alan Jackson	Alicia Keys
Allen Iverson	Ashanti	Ashlee Simpson
Ashton Kutcher	Avril Lavigne	Bernie Mac
Beyoncé	Bow Wow	Britney Spears
Carrie Underwood	Chris Brown	Chris Daughtry
Christina Aguilera	Christopher Paul Curtis	Ciara
Clay Aiken	Condoleezza Rice	Daniel Radcliffe
David Ortiz	Derek Jeter	Eminem
Eve	Fergie (Stacy Ferguson)	50 Cent
Gwen Stefani	Ice Cube	Jamie Foxx
Ja Rule	Jay-Z	Jennifer Lopez
Jessica Simpson	J. K. Rowling	Johnny Depp
JoJo	Justin Berfield	**Justin Timberlake**
Kate Hudson	Keith Urban	Kelly Clarkson
Kenny Chesney	Lance Armstrong	Lindsay Lohan
Mariah Carey	Mario	Mary J. Blige
Mary-Kate and Ashley Olsen	Michael Jackson	Miguel Tejada
Missy Elliott	Nancy Pelosi	Nelly
Orlando Bloom	P. Diddy	Paris Hilton
Peyton Manning	Queen Latifah	Ron Howard
Rudy Giuliani	Sally Field	Selena
Shakira	Shirley Temple	Tim McGraw
Usher	Zac Efron	

Library of Congress Cataloging-in-Publication Data
Tracy, Kathleen.
   Justin Timberlake / by Kathleen Tracy.
      p. cm. — (Blue banner biographies)
   Includes bibliographical references (p.   ), discography (p.   ), filmography (p.   ), and index.
   ISBN 978-1-58415-611-6 (library bound)
   1. Timberlake, Justin, 1981—Juvenile literature. 2. Singers—United States—Biography—Juvenile literature. I. Title.
ML3930.T58T73 2008
782.42164092—dc22
[B]
                                                                    2007019682

ABOUT THE AUTHOR: Kathleen Tracy has been a journalist for over twenty years. Her writing has been featured in magazines including *The Toronto Star's Star Week, A&E's Biography magazine, KidScreen* and *Variety.* She is also the author of numerous biographies and other nonfiction books, including *Mariano Guadalupe Vallejo, William Hewlett: Pioneer of the Computer Age, The Watergate Scandal, The Life and Times of Cicero, Mariah Carey, Kelly Clarkson,* and *The Plymouth Colony: The Pilgrims Settle in New England* for Mitchell Lane Publishers. She divides her time between homes in Studio City and Palm Springs, California.

PHOTO CREDITS: Cover, pp. 4, 23—David Longendyke/Globe Photos; pp. 7, 18, 19—Frank Micelotta/Getty Images; p. 10—Jude Burstein/Globe Photos; p. 14—Getty Images; p. 21—Nina Prommer; p. 25—Mark Allian/Globe Photos; p. 26—Kevin Winter/Getty Images

PPC

CONTENTS

Justin Timberlake would shed his boy band image through the success of his soulful solo albums. "It's an awesome feeling to have that kind of creative control," he says of being on his own, "to feel like you can blossom as an adult, an artist, and a person."

Wardrobe Malfunction

In early 2004 Justin Timberlake's career was red hot. His first solo album, *Justified,* had earned five Grammy nominations. Two of the songs, "Cry Me a River" and "Rock Your Body," were Top Ten hits. He had spent the previous summer touring with Christina Aguilera to sold-out shows. To top it all off, he was going to be performing on one of the world's largest stages: halftime at the Super Bowl.

Ironically, things were going so well and Justin was so busy that when he was first asked to appear at the Super Bowl, he turned the offer down. It wasn't until Janet Jackson called and asked Justin to sing a duet with her that he agreed.

The game was held in Houston on February 1, 2004. Over 89 million Americans and 40 million more viewers in other countries were watching the New England Patriots play the Carolina Panthers. At halftime, Justin headed to the field for what promised to be the biggest, most important performance of his young career.

It ended in disaster.

After Kid Rock, Nelly, and P. Diddy performed, it was time for Justin and Jackson. Their duet was a medley of her "Rhythm Nation" and his "Rock Your Body." As Timberlake sang the last line of his song—*I gotta have you naked by the end of this song*—he grabbed her costume near the shoulder and tugged.

Out popped her right breast. Complete with sun-shaped nipple jewelry.

The show's director quickly cut to a different camera. It happened so fast that five years earlier most people would have wondered if they saw what they thought they saw. But by 2004, thanks to TiVo and other PVRs (personal video recorders), viewers were able to replay the moment over and over . . . and over.

Before you could say *pierced nipple,* the CBS switchboard was besieged with calls from indignant viewers. In the end over 200,000 complaints were lodged. It should be noted, however, that that was only 0.2 percent of the estimated Super Bowl audience. In other words, 99.8 percent didn't complain.

No matter. By the time the game ended, the incident had ignited a political uproar.

Immediately after the performance, Timberlake was unaware of the rising furor. When asked about the incident,

> By the time the game ended, the incident had ignited a political uproar.

Although he was angry that people thought the "wardrobe malfunction" was intentional, Timberlake apologized for his part in the incident. Jackson's career suffered in the fallout, but Timberlake's soared.

he shrugged it off as unintentional. At the post-game *Access Hollywood* party, he joked, "Hey man, we love giving you all something to talk about."

The next day was a different story. "Nipplegate" had become a major political issue. Pro-family and anti-Hollywood activists used the incident as Exhibit A in proving that indecency on TV was out of control.

As a result of the controversy, the National Academy of Recording Arts & Sciences (NARAS), which sponsors the Grammys, announced that Timberlake and Jackson would be banned from the Grammy Awards ceremony being held that week unless they apologized on the air.

Jackson declined and withdrew from the ceremony, but she did issue an official apology, explaining that while it was her idea to have a "costume reveal . . . It was not my intention that it go as far as it did."

Her publicist explained that "the red lace bra under the bustier was supposed to be revealed. There was some kind of collapse in the garment."

Timberlake agreed to apologize at the Grammys. He also apologized prior to the ceremony.

"I am sorry if anyone was offended by the wardrobe malfunction during the halftime performance at the Super Bowl," he said. "It was not intentional and is regrettable."

He was also upset at suggestions that it had been a planned publicity stunt. Justin had only learned of the costume reveal right before the show.

"I don't wanna be involved in a stunt, that's not my style," he said, adding, "I was completely shocked and appalled, and all I could say was 'Oh my God, Oh my God.' "

> *"I was completely shocked and appalled, and all I could say was 'Oh my God, Oh my God.' "*

Americans were divided on the issue of whether or not baring a breast during a performance was truly indecent—or simply of questionable taste. Polls taken at the time indicated that the majority of viewers felt such adult-oriented entertainment was inappropriate during a family show but stopped short of calling it indecent.

The Federal Communications Commission (FCC), however, disagreed and levied a $550,000 fine against the network. CBS appealed, and three years later, the outcome remained undecided.

For Timberlake, it was a humbling experience. He realized how quickly fortunes can change. Some music industry observers wondered if his career could survive the controversy.

Not only would his career survive, it would flourish.

A Born Singer

Few American cities have the rich musical heritage of Memphis, Tennessee. From gospel to Elvis to the Gibson guitar manufacturing plant, Memphis's history is set to a rock and blues beat. It seems particularly fitting that Justin Randall Timberlake was born there on January 31, 1981.

Justin's mother, Lynn Bomar, was only twenty years old when she gave birth to Justin. His dad, Randall Timberlake, sang harmony and played bass guitar in a bluegrass band with Lynn's brother. Even at an early age, it was clear that Justin had inherited his father's musical talents.

"When Justin was a little-bitty baby, like three or four months old, we'd sit him in those seats, like a car seat, on the kitchen counter," Lynn recalls. "He'd kick his legs to the beat of the music. We'd change the music and he'd kick his legs to the new beat. We'd say to our friends, 'Dude! Look at this!' He was like a little toy."

It wasn't long before he began singing along.

Timberlake credits his hometown for influencing his musical tastes. "Memphis is the blues capital of the world. . . . I remember going down to Beale Street . . . and listening to those soulful voices come out of those bars."

"We were coming home from a bluegrass festival in Mississippi with my brother and sister-in-law and all of a sudden my brother said, 'Is anyone listening to him?' Justin was adding a harmony to the songs on the radio. He was freakin' two!"

His parents divorced when he was two, and Lynn married a banker named Paul Harless three years later. Justin told *GQ* that his stepfather "has been the guiding force. Maybe not in my career, but in how to behave as a human being."

Randall Timberlake also eventually remarried, and from that marriage Justin has two half brothers, Jonathan and Stephen.

While researching his family tree, Justin discovered that he is of British descent—and part American Indian. "There was a British lad who was in a war, not sure which war, but he ran away from the war because he fell in love with an Indian girl, and that's where my family tree started," he explains.

Justin grew up in Millington, a small town about a twenty-five-minute car ride from Memphis. He attended E. E. Jeter Elementary School and played on the school basketball team—but the future teen idol was anything *but* a heartthrob as a kid.

"I had really awkward hair and terrible skin and I was really scrawny. I looked like a broccolini . . . because I was long and skinny. I was a really weird-looking kid!"

Even then Justin knew what he wanted to be in life.

"Honestly, ever since I was a really little boy I always sang. So I figured out that that was sort of my calling. I didn't really have to think about it because I knew it was always there, that it's what I should be doing."

He honed his skills by singing in church—his grandfather was a Baptist minister—and entering as many talent contests as he could find.

When Justin was eleven, his mother took him to an open audition being held in Nashville for the television talent show *Star Search*. He was selected and was flown to Los Angeles to compete. Going by the name Justin Randall, he sang country songs—while wearing a cowboy hat and fringed shirt. Although he didn't win, Justin was proud of his performance. More importantly, the show marked the start of his professional career.

> **"I had really awkward hair and terrible skin and I was really scrawny. I looked like a broccolini."**

As always, his mom was his biggest supporter. They continue to share an exceptionally close relationship.

"She . . . taught me how to be who I am," Timberlake told *Rolling Stone.* "Whatever I needed to further myself,

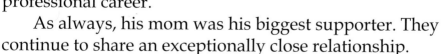

she's always been there to give it. . . . And if she thought it was too much, she'd say something. She's been my best friend since I figured out who I wanted to be. She's great, and such a fun woman."

> ### "I was a tortured young dude—to the point of rage . . . I wanted everything to be perfect."

Justin admitted to *Entertainment Weekly* that he was often less than entertaining company in his preteen years. "I was a tortured young dude—to the point of rage." He says he would stare at the ground scowling much of the time. "My mom makes jokes, 'It's no shock to me you're obsessed with sneakers because that's the only thing you looked at for the first ten years of your life.' And if I couldn't do something really well when I was a kid, I wouldn't do it at all. I wanted everything to be perfect."

Which is why Lynn made sure that her son knew he could quit anytime he wanted.

"It was always like, 'Justin, tell me if you don't want to do this,'" he recalls. "And I was like, 'Mom, this is what I really love to do.'"

In 1993, a year after appearing on *Star Search,* Justin finally got the break he'd been waiting for. He was cast in the sixth season of Disney's *The All New Mickey Mouse Club,* usually referred to as *MMC.*

Not only would the show give him a chance to perform in front of a national audience every day, he would also meet his first love there.

M-I-C-K-E-Y M-O-U-S-E

*T*he original *Mickey Mouse Club* series aired from 1955 to 1959. An updated version in 1977 flopped and was canceled after a few months. The Disney Channel revamped the series in 1989 for cable and it became a hit with preteen audiences. *MMC* featured comedy skits, an ongoing soap opera called *Emerald Cove,* and lots of music, so Justin was able to show off both his acting and his singing skills.

The show filmed in Orlando, Florida, at the Disney-MGM Studios. Since they were all away from home, the young Mouseketeers became good friends. Among Justin's cast mates were Christina Aguilera, Britney Spears, and JC Chasez. Being on *MMC* was the greatest professional achievement of Justin's life at that point. When he left the show after it was canceled, he became depressed. He'd find himself crying but not know why.

That was also a hard time for Justin for another reason.

"School was kind of tough on me," he admitted in an online interview, "because I had to go back and forth from

Justin's first big break was being cast in the All New Mickey Mouse Club (MMC). *Disney's kid-oriented variety show featured some of pop music's biggest future stars, including Britney Spears (seated, right), Christina Aguilera (standing, right), and Justin (standing, right). Justin's future band mate JC Chasez was also in the cast (standing, left).*

homeschool when I was on the *Mickey Mouse Club* to regular school. So was being back after being absent so long . . . That was the hardest thing—I was never in one place for that time."

Instead of going to high school, Justin was tutored so that he could pursue a music career. While in Nashville recording some songs during 1995, Timberlake was contacted by a singer named Chris Kirkpatrick. He was putting a vocal group together and invited Justin to join them. In turn, Justin suggested his *MMC* friend JC Chasez. Also recruited was Joey Fatone, who was a well-known performer in the Orlando area. Rounding out the group was Lance Bass, who studied with Justin's vocal coach.

Later, when some critics dismissed the group as another manufactured boy band, Timberlake would take issue.

"The main thing you should understand about how we got together is that there was no record company involved or management team," Justin told the *Denver Post*. "We were the ones who did it."

While the guys worked on their sound, they often hung out at Lynn's Orlando home, getting to know one another. Justin's mom is the one who came up with 'NSync as the group's name; after hearing them sing together, she noted how in sync they were with one another.

It wasn't long before the group found a manager—Lou Pearlman, who had also worked with New Kids on the Block and Backstreet Boys—and was signed to a record deal. At just fourteen, Timberlake had reached his goal—and admits he didn't handle it well.

"I thought I was the coolest guy. You couldn't talk to me. Nobody could tell me anything. I'd be like, 'I have a record contract!' "

'NSync did have a record contract, but it would be a while before anyone in America knew it.

> *"I thought I was the coolest guy. You couldn't talk to me. Nobody could tell me anything. I'd be like, 'I have a record contract!' "*

Their first record deal was signed in Germany. The resulting album, **NSYNC*, generated two hit singles—"Tearing Up My Heart" and "I Want You Back." After touring extensively in Europe and Asia, they returned to America and signed with RCA. The album was released in the U.S. in March 1998. Aiming for the teen crowd, the group toured roller skating rinks and was featured in some concert specials on the Disney Channel. In October 1998 they joined Janet Jackson's tour for two weeks as her opening act. The hard work was paying off.

By early 1999, 'NSync had sold over 5 million albums—their Christmas album sold another million—and were ready to go on their own tour. Although he was the youngest, Justin often came across as the group's front man. "We're like brothers. We're like friends. We get along."

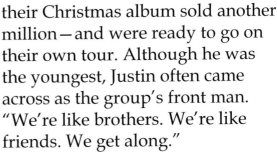

"If you want to do something that you love to do, you make sacrifices to do it. And that's what I've done."

When asked about his dance moves, Timberlake said he just did what came naturally. "I've taken maybe one class before, and it was a hip-hop class. I've never taken any technical dance lessons. I've always just picked up moves from watching, like, Janet Jackson on television."

He also dismissed concerns that he was missing out by working so much.

"If you want to do something that you love to do, you make sacrifices to do it. And that's what I've done. Everybody always asks, 'Do you regret missing your teenage years?' But I haven't missed anything. I've gained so much more that a lot of people can't have. I don't regret anything, because this is what I love to do, and I'm happy that I found this out at such an early age."

He would also find out that being successful sometimes came with a dark side.

American Teen Idol

*D*espite their surging popularity and booming record sales, the members of 'NSync were not happy. They felt that their manager, Lou Pearlman, was cheating them. Because he was getting paid as both their manager and as their record producer, he was allegedly taking an unacceptably high percentage of their earnings. They claimed that of the more than $10 million they had earned from touring and sales, the group had received only $300,000 — or about three percent. They decided to fire Pearlman and switch record labels for their next album.

In October 1999, Pearlman claimed that the members of 'NSync had breached their contract with him. He filed a $150-million lawsuit against the group and their new label, Jive Records. The suit also sought to prevent the group from using the name 'NSync. Pearlman's lawyer went on MTV and admitted he was seeking "to obtain a court order to prevent 'NSync from existing."

So was their breakup three and a half years later, in March 2002.

Although Timberlake won't confirm that the couple broke up over her secretly dating choreographer Wade Robson—who was a friend of Justin's—he does admit she broke his heart. He says she was the third girl to do so.

> *"I'm a very loving, caring person and if I start dating you . . . it may take me a long time to give myself away to you, but once I do, that's it."*

"I was fifteen the first time. She cheated on me and I broke up with her. I'd been going with her for a year. The second one I saw for a year and a half. . . . They've all gone down the same way. All of them . . . I mean, she [Britney] has a beautiful heart, but if I've lost trust in someone, I don't think it's right for me to be with them.

"I'm a very loving, caring person and if I start dating you . . . it may take me a long time to give myself away to you, but once I do, that's it."

His mother was equally upset over the breakup. "Britney grew up on my living room floor. I still love her to death. They had, from day one, instant chemistry between them. She's a sweet girl."

Justin used the experience and his heartache as inspiration for writing "Cry Me a River," but the song wasn't for an 'NSync album. After seven years, the five friends were ready to try other things. Timberlake was now a grown man who wanted to flex his musical muscles as a

After seven successful years together, the members of 'NSync went their separate ways. From left to right: JC Chasez, Justin Timberlake, Joey Fatone, Chris Kirkpatrick, and Lance Bass.

solo artist. In late 2002 he released *Justified,* which went on to sell over 5 million copies and allowed Justin to present himself as more of an adult.

He also started dating and was linked with actress Jenna Dewan and *Charmed* star Alyssa Milano. At the time he commented, "I think I'm in this zone where I don't want to be attached to anyone."

His bachelor days ended abruptly in April 2003 after meeting Cameron Diaz at the Nickelodeon Kids' Choice Awards. In a surprising turn of events, Justin did something nobody could have predicted.

Bringing Sexy Back

*J*ustin was twenty-three years old and had been working for almost half his life.

"I was burnt," he admitted to *Rolling Stone.* "My dad was like, 'You should enjoy your life—one day you're gonna be my age and you'll want to do things that you should have done when you had the body to do them.'

"I was like, 'Damn, you're right!'"

So he took a musical time-out. "When I took two years off, I was like, 'Oh, s***! This is what the world looks like at a regular pace.' That was amazing for me. Just the little things, like sitting home on the weekend or making a Sunday tee time. Play golf, then come back home, have a beer and call it a day."

A natural athlete, he also went snowboarding, hiked in the mountains near his Los Angeles home with his two boxers, Buckley and Brennan, and took off for Hawaii to surf. Diaz was never far away—and neither were the

For Justin, the downside of success is the loss of privacy and constantly being in the media spotlight. "Sometimes you just want your life to be your life, not everybody else's to speculate on. As far as the press is concerned, they're going to say what they want to say. . . . Probably about ten to fifteen percent of the time it's accurate."

paparazzi—but Timberlake had learned to cope with media attention by ignoring it.

"You sort of know it exists. . . . But if I wasn't doing all this promotion I wouldn't even know about it. I'd be surfing or snowboarding or playing golf," he told *Rolling Stone*. "That's how I keep my sanity. You cannot do this without a sense of humor."

In October 2003, he agreed to host *Saturday Night Live*. The skits showed both Justin's sense of humor and his acting ability. Not long after, he started getting acting offers. Then, after the February 2004 fiasco at the Super Bowl, Timberlake was ready to give acting a serious try.

"The reason I got into film is because I needed something inspiring, but more intimate, that I didn't have to do in front of 18,000 people every night."

During his self-imposed hiatus from music, Justin appeared in four movies, including providing the voice of Artie for *Shrek the Third* opposite Diaz. But it was the edgy *Alpha Dog* that earned Justin his best reviews. The film, which costars Bruce Willis and premiered in January 2007, is based on an actual Los Angeles murder. In the movie, Timberlake plays a gangbanger with a sensitive side.

> **"The reason I got into film is because I needed something inspiring, but more intimate, that I didn't have to do in front of 18,000 people every night."**

"Justin's got such an easy way of moving," says the film's director, Nick Cassavetes, "much like a young [John] Travolta in *Saturday Night Fever*."

In between acting gigs, Justin would do "guest work" on others' albums, such as singing background on the Black Eyed Peas' "Where Is the Love?" While recording "Signs" with Snoop Dogg in May 2005, Justin's throat didn't feel right. He was diagnosed with nodules that required surgical removal. After the operation, Timberlake wasn't allowed to sing or even talk above a whisper until he was completely healed. He took the opportunity of the unexpected hiatus that summer to form his own record label, JayTee Records.

When he was cleared to go back to work, a refreshed Justin was ready. The break from music was the best thing

Justin shows off some of his famous breakdance moves on his 2003 tour for Justified. *In addition to his natural singing ability, Timberlake was born with an innate sense of rhythm. "I never took formal dance training. It's something I picked up from going to clubs and watching MTV."*

creatively he could have done. He was eager to get back to the recording studio and work on a new album—and a new sound.

"I knew that I needed something new," he explained to writer Austin Scaggs. "I wanted to take more of a chance—experiment. I said to myself, 'I don't want anything I do to sound like *that*,'" referring to what he was hearing on Top 40 radio. "I just didn't think it was that good."

He started working on his new album in December 2005. *FutureSex/LoveSounds* was released in September 2006. His single "SexyBack" was released earlier, in July, and despite concern by Jive Records executives that the song wasn't Justin's expected style, it eventually spent seven weeks at number one on Billboard's Hot 100.

Justin performs at Nickelodeon's 20th Annual Kids' Choice Awards in 2007, an event he also hosted. That year, the two-time Burp Award–winner finally met his match. Timberlake was bested by an ensemble burp by all the kids in the audience.

Justin was now not only successful, he had earned the respect of critics and fans alike for being so much more than some boy-band singer. He was an innovator with a talent that ensured a long career.

He was also a young man who believed in giving back. He uses his celebrity to help children and to protect nature. In 2001, he founded the Justin Timberlake Foundation, which offers monetary grants to school and community music programs. Representatives from his foundation have lobbied for increased government funding for music education. Justin also supports Childwatch, which works to prevent child abductions, and Wildlife Warriors Worldwide, founded by the late Steve Irwin.

In December 2006, Timberlake broke up with Cameron Diaz and issued an official statement: "We have, in fact, ended our romantic relationship and have done so mutually and as friends, with continued love and respect for one another."

"Regardless of whether you want to be a singer, doctor or lawyer, learn all you can about it. Then if you give 150 percent, you'll get a 100 percent outcome."

Justin has started dating again but typically believes a gentleman should never kiss and tell. He's also old enough now to offer a simple perspective on what it takes to achieve your dreams. "Regardless of whether you want to be a singer, doctor or lawyer, learn all you can about it. Then if you give 150 percent, you'll get a 100 percent outcome."

CHRONOLOGY

1981   Justin Randall Timberlake is born on January 31 in Memphis, Tennessee.

1992   At the age of eleven, Justin appears on *Star Search*.

1993   He is cast on *The All New Mickey Mouse Club*.

1995   He joins the band 'NSync.

1998   'NSync's first album is released in March.

1999   Along with bandmates, Justin fires manager Lou Pearlman and changes record labels. He begins dating Britney Spears.

2000   A third 'NSync album, *No Strings Attached*, is released in March.

2001   *Celebrity* is released in July; Justin starts the Justin Timberlake Foundation.

2002   Justin breaks up with Spears in March. He releases *Justified*, his first solo album, in November.

2003   Justin gets *Punk'd* by Ashton Kutcher on the MTV series, and meets Cameron Diaz at the Nickelodeon Kids' Choice Awards.

2004   He performs with Janet Jackson at the Super Bowl halftime show. A week later, he wins Grammys for best pop vocal album and best male pop vocal performance.

2005   He establishes his own record label, JayTee Records, and makes film debut in *Edison Force*.

2006   Justin releases "SexyBack" single in July, and second solo album, *FutureSex/LoveSounds*, in September. With best friend, Trace Ayala, he starts a clothing line, William Rast.

2007   Justin wins two more Grammys in February. In March, he hosts the 20th Annual Nickelodeon Kids' Choice Awards.

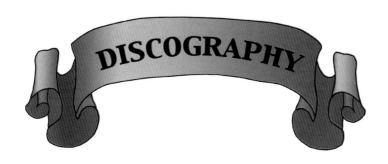

DISCOGRAPHY

Solo

2006　*FutureSex/LoveSounds*

2002　*Justified*

With 'NSync

2005　*Greatest Hits*

2001　*Celebrity*

2000　*No Strings Attached*

1998　*NSYNC* and *Home for Christmas*

1998　*Home for Christmas*

FILMOGRAPHY

2007　*Shrek the Third* (voice)

2006　*Black Snake Moan*

2006　*Alpha Dog*

2005　*Edison Force*

2001　*On the Line*

2000　*Longshot*

2000　*Model Behavior* (TV movie)

1999　*Touched By an Angel* (TV series — guest spot)

FURTHER READING

Books

Black, Susan, and Justin Timberlake. *Justin Timberlake: "Talking."* New York: Omnibus Press, 2004.

Roach, Martin. *Justin Timberlake: The Unofficial Book*. New York: Virgin Books, 2003.

Smith, Sean. *Justin: The Unauthorized Biography*. New York: Pocket Books, 2005.

Works Consulted

CBS News: *Entertainment,* "Justin: Breast Shocked Me, Too" http://www.cbsnews.com/stories/2004/02/05/entertainment/main598191.shtml

CNN: *Entertainment,* "Jackson Overexposure: TV Feels Heat" http://www.cnn.com/2004/SHOWBIZ/TV/02/05/superbowl.jackson/

CNN: *U.S.,* "Apologetic Jackson Says 'Costume Reveal' Went Awry" http://www.cnn.com/2004/US/02/02/superbowl.jackson

Faded Youth: *Wednesday, October 25, 2006,* "Justin Timberlake Does British *GQ*" http://fadedyouth.blogspot.com/2006/10/justin-timberlake-does-british-gq.html

GMTV: *Entertainment Today,* "Showbiz Exclusives—Justin's Secret" http://www.gm.tv/index.cfm?articleid=21993

Guardian Unlimited: *Observer Mail*, "Justin Timberlake Interview"
  http://observer.guardian.co.uk/observermail/story/
  0,,1820595,00.html

Harden, Mark. " 'Nstant Stardom: 'NSync's Street-savvy Sound Rides
  Youth Wave." *The Denver Post*. January 8, 1999.

Klueber, Jillian. *Kid Scoops*, "Justin's Solo Act"
  http://www.timeforkids.com/TFK/kidscoops/story/
  0,14989,389161,00.html

Oldenburg, Ann. *Super Bowl XXXVIII*, "Jackson's Halftime Stunt Fuels
  Indecency Debate"
  http://www.usatoday.com/sports/football/super/2004-02-02-
  jackson-halftime-incident_x.htm

People: *News*, "Justin Timberlake and Cameron Diaz Break Up"
  http://www.people.com/people/article/0,,1142562,00.html

Rosen, Craig. *Y! Music News*, " 'NSync Trans Con War of Words Heating
  Up" http://music.yahoo.com/read/news/12040290

Scaggs, Austin. "Justin Timberlake Revs Up His Sex Machine"
  http://www.rollingstone.com/news/story/11514699/
  justin_timberlake_revs_up_his_sex_machine

On the Internet

American Music Conference: *The Justin Timberlake Foundation*
  http://www.amc-music.com/partners/timberlake.htm

Jive Records: *Justin Timberlake*
  http://www.justintimberlake.com

MySpace: *Justin Timberlake*
  http://www.myspace.com/justintimberlake

INDEX